Children
of the Bible

Margaret McAllister

ILLUSTRATED BY
Alida Massari

LION
CHILDREN'S

For Connie Bush   M.M.
For my little girl, Diana   A.M.

Text copyright © 2017 Margaret McAllister
Illustrations copyright © 2017 Alida Massari
This edition copyright © 2019 Lion Hudson IP Limited

The right of Margaret McAllister to be identified as the author and of Alida Massari to be identified as the illustrator of this work has been asserted by them in accordance with the Copyright, Designs and Patents Act 1988.

All rights reserved. No part of this publication may be reproduced or transmitted in any form or by any means, electronic or mechanical, including photocopy, recording, or any information storage and retrieval system, without permission in writing from the publisher.

Published by
Lion Hudson Limited
Wilkinson House, Jordan Hill Business Park,
Banbury Road, Oxford OX2 8DR, England
www.lionhudson.com

ISBN 978 0 7459 7829 1

First edition 2019

A catalogue record for this book is available from the British Library

Printed and bound in Malaysia, February 2019, LH18

Contents

Samuel   4
1 Samuel 1–3

David   9
1 Samuel 17

Elijah and the Widow's Son   13
1 Kings 16–17

Elisha and the Boy from Shunem   17
2 Kings 4

The Baby in the Temple   21
Luke 2

Blessing the Children   25
Mark 10; Matthew 19

Beth, Daughter of Jairus   28
Mark 5; Luke 8; Matthew 9

Bread and Fishes   33
Matthew 14; Luke 9; John 6

The Child in the Middle   39
Matthew 18

Helen, the Jailer's Daughter   44
Acts 16

Samuel

The laws God gave to our people were written on a scroll. The scroll was kept in the sacred wooden box called the ark of the covenant, which had two carved wooden angels on the top and long wooden poles for carrying it around. The ark was in the tabernacle: a tent like the ones our people lived in when they had no homeland and were wanderers. The tabernacle was in the shrine at Shiloh, a big, solidly made building with a courtyard where people came to worship. So – the scroll was in the ark, the ark was in the tabernacle, the tabernacle was in the shrine, and somewhere in all that was my big brother Samuel. When he knew we were coming to visit he'd be outside, looking for us.

There was a reason why Samuel lived at Shiloh, not at home with the rest of us. I heard the story from my family. It was like this. Before any of us were born, my father had two wives, Peninnah and Hannah. In those days Peninnah had lots of children and Hannah had none, which broke her heart, even though my father loved her dearly. Every year they'd go on pilgrimage to Shiloh, and Hannah always felt that everybody was noticing them and thinking, "look at that woman with all those lovely children! Isn't it strange that the other wife doesn't have any?"

One evening after dinner, Hannah was so upset that she ran from the house and didn't stop running until she got to the shrine. (I think Peninnah had upset her.) At the shrine she dropped to her knees and prayed silently, begging God for a child. Eli, the old priest, was there, and he must have wondered what this woman was doing, kneeling there with her lips moving and no sound coming out. He thought she was drunk! But when Hannah explained to him that she was pouring out her heart to God he was kind, and gave her his blessing. Perhaps he prayed for her, too. Anyway, she did have a baby! And that baby was my brother Samuel.

She was so happy to have him, you'd think she'd never let him out of her sight, wouldn't you? But she was so grateful for this little boy that she promised to offer him to serve God. (We're a Levite family so Samuel would have been a priest sooner or later, but this was sooner.) He was barely two when she took him to the shrine and left him in Eli's care. It wasn't just Eli – there were women who helped at the shrine, cooking, welcoming pilgrims and so on, and I think they all fussed over Samuel and mothered him.

I was born after Samuel and I can't remember him ever living at home, but I loved going to visit him. We'd all go once a year and stay for a few days. By all of us I mean me, Ma (Hannah) and Dad, my three younger brothers and my little sister Sara. Ma always gave Samuel a new tunic, and of course each year the tunics got bigger. Samuel would rush into her arms as soon as he saw her, and then he and I would run off together and spend every moment playing and hiding from Eli. We hid from his grown up sons, too – Hophni and Phinehas – because we didn't like them. Nobody did. They were trouble, always chasing the women and helping themselves to the offerings the pilgrims brought, and Eli couldn't do anything about them.

There was one year when we went to visit Samuel and I knew at once that he'd changed. Suddenly he seemed very grown up and a bit solemn, and I knew there was something bothering him, so I asked him. This is what he told me, as we sat on the wall and looked over at the vineyard.

"It was my turn to sleep in the shrine, on a mat in front of the ark of the covenant," he said. "It's lonely and a bit uncomfortable, but I don't mind because it feels… it feels safe, just me and the lamplight, and knowing that God's there too. Anyway, I was just falling asleep when I heard somebody calling me. I thought it must be Eli so I got up and went to see what he wanted, but he said it wasn't him. I thought I must have been dreaming, so I went back to bed – then I heard the voice again, and I *knew* I'd heard it. It had to be Eli, it couldn't be anyone else, so I got up again and went to him. I was a bit scared that he'd be cross about being woken up twice in one night, but he just…" he paused, then went on, "however I say this, it's going to sound all wrong."

"Go on," I said.

"Well, what happened was," he said, "Eli told me that there was only one voice it could be. He said I had to go back to my mat, and if the voice called me again I had to say, 'Speak, Lord, for your servant is listening.'"

"What!" I said and clapped my hands to my mouth. *Lord?* Could he really mean…?

"I went back to bed," Samuel went on. "The voice came again, so I sat up and said the words Eli had told me to say – 'Speak, Lord, for your servant is listening.' Then he spoke to me."

I'd heard of God speaking to people before, but that was in the days when he spoke to our ancestor Abraham and our great leader Moses, and other people like that. God speaking to a boy seemed impossible, but I only had to look at Samuel to know he was telling the truth.

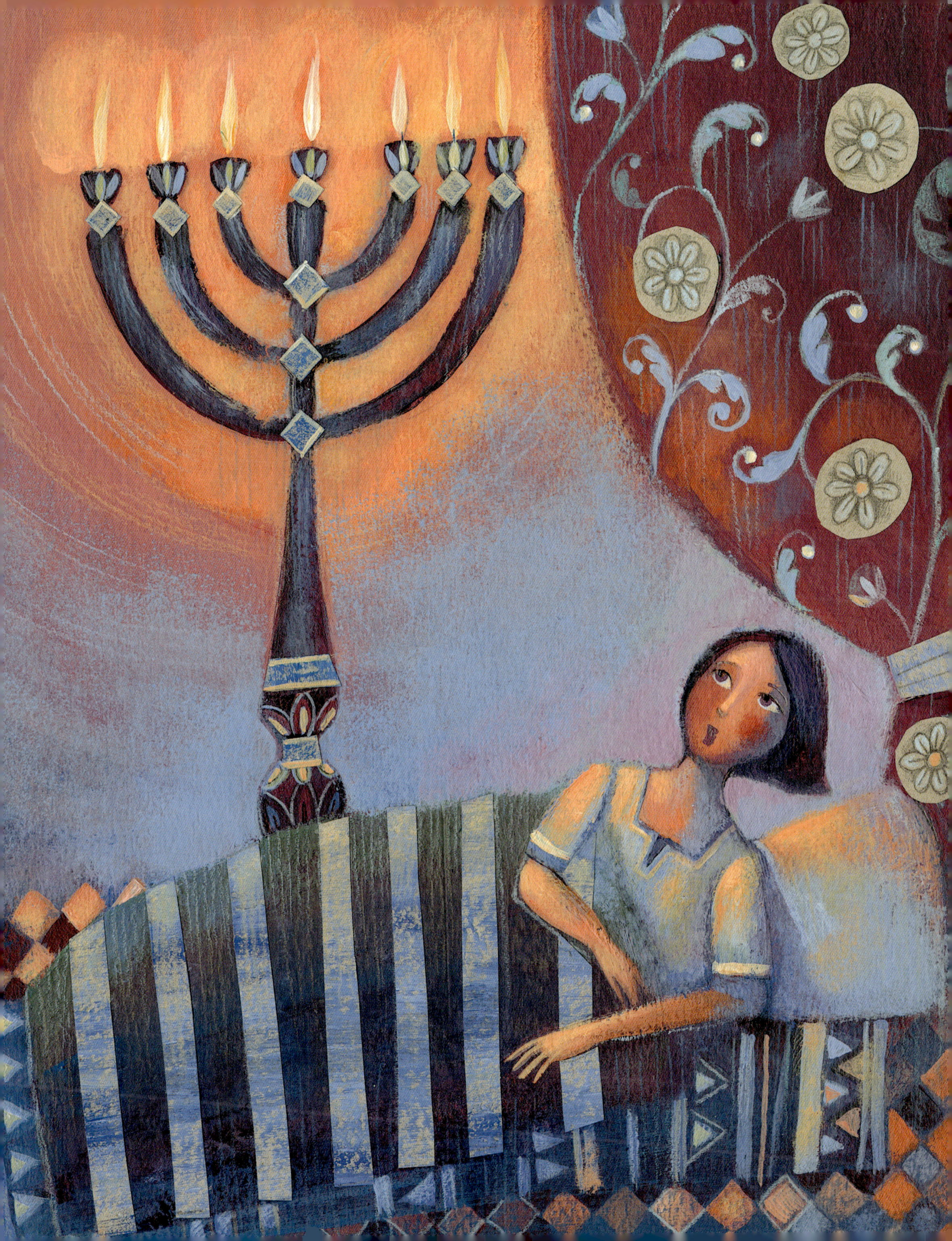

"I heard him," he said. "I don't know why he told me, but he gave me a message for Eli. I sort of wish he hadn't. The message was, Hophni and Phinehas are such a disgrace that he doesn't want them to do any more damage. Eli's whole family will be swept away, and they won't be priests any more."

"Did you tell Eli?" I asked.

"I had to," Samuel said. "And I think he expected it, because he just said, 'God will do what he knows is best.'"

At that point I nearly asked Samuel – if Eli's family aren't going to lead and guide us, who will? But then I realized the answer to that. I could tell that Samuel knew, too. No wonder he'd changed.

Samuel became priest, prophet, and judge of Israel, and guided the whole nation. The time came when the people of Israel wanted a king. Samuel didn't like this idea at all but they insisted, so he asked for God's guidance. He anointed Saul as the first king, and then David.

David

Are you the youngest in your family? If you are, do you ever feel that the rest of them try to keep you a baby? Do you feel as if they can't let you grow up? They probably don't mean to, but they do it all the same.

It was like that for me. I was the youngest of eight boys, and when Israel was at war against the Philistines three of my older brothers went to join the army. I wanted to go too, but they said I was too young and I had to stay at home and look after the sheep.

Sheep, yes! I used to think that God must have made sheep because cows were too exciting – but then I discovered that sometimes shepherding did get exciting, very exciting, when wild animals threatened my flock and all I had to protect them was a few stones and a slingshot. I was the one who stood between a lion and a lamb. But I still wanted to be a soldier.

Some chance! In those days, the nearest I ever got to the front line was taking my brothers their dinner. Our army led by King Saul had camped at one side of a valley, with the Philistines at the other.

I wanted to do something brave and great so that my brothers would admire me. At the same time, I had a feeling that it wouldn't matter if I turned out to be the best warrior since Gideon or a prophet as great as Samuel, it wouldn't make a difference. I could be the King of Israel; they'd still see me as their kid brother.

However one day I was taking food to my brothers, when I heard our soldiers talking about someone called Goliath and I asked them who he was. I found out that Goliath was the Philistines' champion: a giant of a man who strode out from the camp every day and challenged the Israelites to single combat. (That means that instead of everyone going into battle, two warriors fight it out between them and the winner's side wins the whole war!) Nobody would fight Goliath. He had a spear even taller than he was and a javelin slung across his back, and his armour was solid bronze so nothing could get through it. Every day he stood shouting insults against us and our God. He knew that nobody would fight him, but he enjoyed getting on our army's nerves with his bragging and swearing.

My brothers were pleased to see the food, but not me. They just wanted me to hand it over and push off home, and they were angry with me for questioning the soldiers about Goliath.

What was the matter with asking questions? How else would I find out? And more importantly, why should Goliath be allowed to get away with it?

I wasn't a soldier. I was a shepherd, but a shepherd has to look after himself and his flock. Didn't I tell you about the wild animals? Standing between a lion and a lamb? That's what I said to King Saul when I went to his tent and told him I wanted to fight Goliath. Our God had kept me safe from the wild animals and I reckoned he could protect me from a bully with a spear, too.

King Saul eventually agreed to let me fight Goliath. He even offered me his own armour to wear, but it was big and heavy and I couldn't even walk in it, so I took it off. The sword weighed me down, too, and anyway I didn't plan to get close enough to Goliath to need one. I had my shepherd's sling, and chose five smooth pebbles from the brook. These were the weapons I was skilled with.

Goliath saw me coming. He swore at me in the name of his god and said he was going to feed me to the birds.

"God will give you into my hands," I shouted. "Everyone will see that our

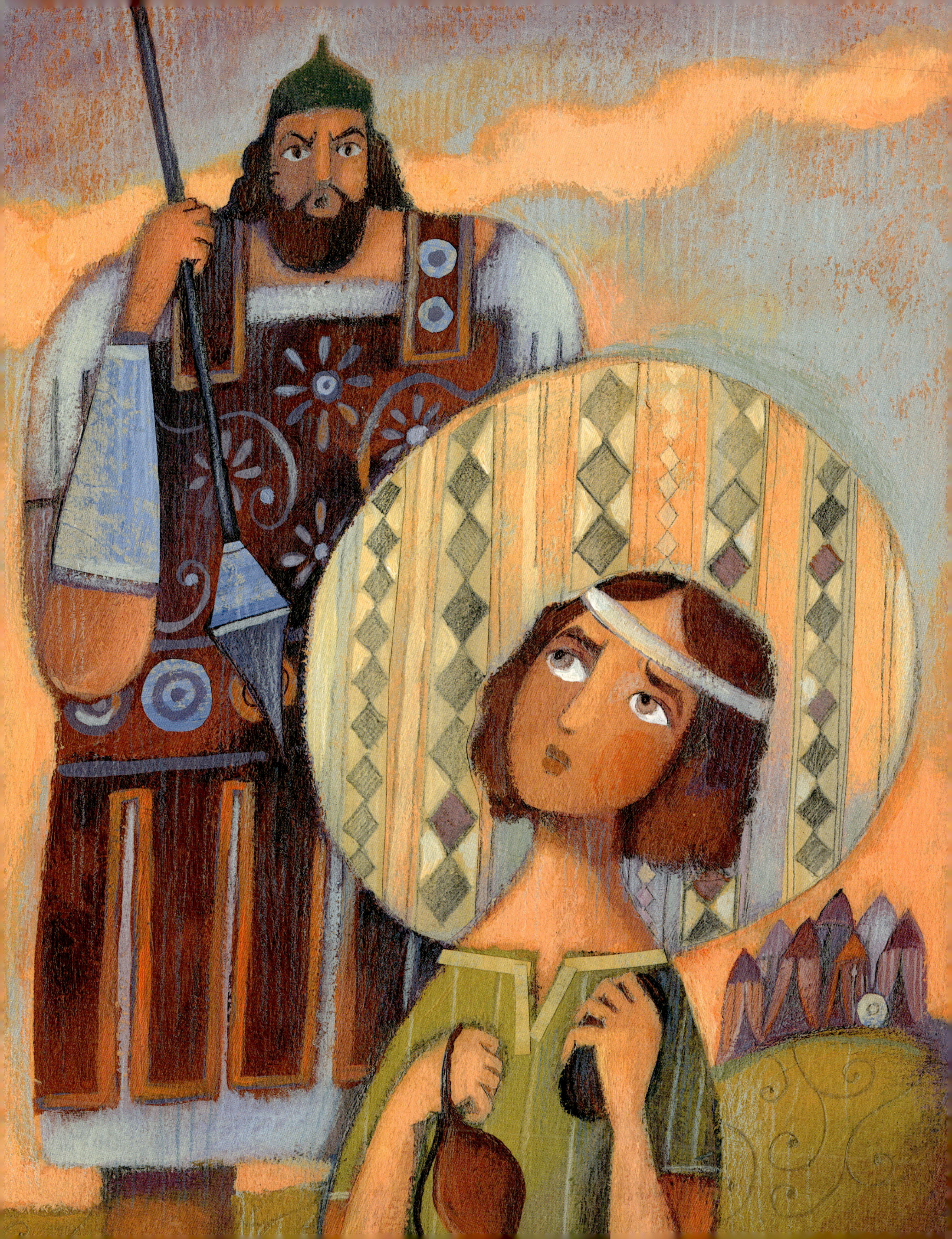

God doesn't need swords and shields."

He marched steadily to meet me and I knew he meant to look so terrifying that I'd run away. I did run: I ran toward him, and when the distance was right I fitted a stone into the sling, swung it, and launched it right at his forehead. I'm a good shot. It hit him hard between the eyes and he crumpled down like a puppet! The Philistines were so shocked that they turned and fled, with our army cheering and shouting as they ran after them.

Even my brothers were impressed and King Saul was delighted that Goliath was dead, so it should have been happy ever after, but it wasn't the end at all. It was a beginning. Suddenly I wasn't just somebody's kid brother. I was the hero of the day, everyone was talking about me, and King Saul was jealous. From that day on, he suspected me of trying to take over the kingdom.

That was the beginning of my story.

David was soon very popular and married Saul's daughter Michal. He became the best friend of Saul's son Jonathan, and led Saul's armies in battle. Saul was then insanely jealous and wanted to kill him, so David had to escape and live as an outlaw. Without David to lead them, Israel's armies were later defeated in a battle in which Saul and Jonathan were killed. David became king, and was the most famous of all Israel's kings. Books 1 and 2 Samuel are full of David's adventures, achievements, and mistakes – yes, he made those too!

Elijah and the Widow's Son

He was Elijah the Prophet, the greatest prophet in Israel, and a hero. He was the one who stood up to the weak King Ahab and the ruthless Queen Jezebel. When Jezebel tried to destroy the religion of Israel, Elijah protected the prophets. It was even said that God spoke to Elijah.

Oh yes, God spoke to Elijah. As far as Elijah was concerned, this meant that God was always telling him to do impossible things! He knew that it would really be God doing the impossible things through him – but that meant having faith, a lot of faith. Sometimes, it seemed as if God only turned up at the last minute. It wasn't easy being the greatest prophet in Israel.

Firstly, God told Elijah to warn King Ahab that there would be no more rainfall for two or three years. People would go hungry. After that, Elijah was to go to a place in Cherith, where there was a brook. He'd have water from the brook even in the drought, and ravens would bring him food. They did, but at last the brook dried up.

"Go to Zarephath, near Sidon," God told him. "You'll meet a poor widow there. I've told her to feed you."

As usual, Elijah trudged away and did as God required. He finally arrived in

Zarephath, saw a poor woman collecting firewood, and asked her for a drink of water. "And may I have some bread, too?" he asked.

"Sir, I haven't any to give," she said, and as she spoke he noticed how thin her face was. "I have just enough flour and oil to make a little bread for my son and me, if I can gather enough wood for a fire to cook it on. When that last bread is finished I don't know what we'll do." Tears welled in her eyes. "I suppose we'll starve."

"Then please go and prepare your bread," said Elijah, "but before you eat, bring me some, because God has made this clear to me — the bowl won't run out of flour and the jar won't run out of oil before the rains come again."

Elijah was used to God asking him to do the impossible, but this was different. He was the one asking somebody else to do the impossible, and not just anyone — a penniless woman with a hungry child. This time, was God just asking too much?

However, the woman went home, made the bread, and brought it to Elijah, and just as he had said there was enough for her son and herself too. The flour bowl should have been empty after that, but the next day it was full again... and the next! Day after day there was flour in the bowl and oil in the jar, and they always had bread to eat. But not everything went smoothly.

One morning the widow's son became poorly, and in a short time he was seriously unwell. His mother did her best, as mothers do. She nursed and cared, hoped and prayed, but to her terrible distress, the boy died. She gathered his body in her arms and carried him to Elijah.

"Man of God!" she cried. "Why has this happened? Have you been telling God of my sins, so that he's destroyed my boy?"

Elijah didn't try to reason with her or console her. He took the child, carried him upstairs, laid him on the bed, and shouted at God.

"Why have you done this?" he cried. "Haven't you seen how faithful this woman is, and you take her son away from her?"

Then he stopped shouting and began to pray. God was always asking him to do the impossible, and with God's help, he always did it. Three times Elijah tried to revive the child.

"Please, Lord," he prayed. "Put life back into this child!"

Suddenly the boy took a breath, and went on breathing. Warmth came back into his face. His pulse grew strong and steady. Elijah carried him downstairs, and put him into his mother's arms.

"You really are a man of God!" she said. "And God speaks through you!"

The story in the Bible doesn't tell any more about the widow and her son. It does go on to tell us about Elijah, listening to God, and having to do the impossible, time and time again.

Elijah went on challenging the rulers of the country and keeping the people of Israel faithful to God. In a dramatic meeting with Jezebel's priests, he demonstrated God's great power, and Jezebel vowed to kill him. He chose Elisha to be his disciple and trained him to take over from him, and was at last carried to heaven in a fiery chariot.

Elisha and the Boy from Shunem

After the prophet Elijah came Elisha. As the most respected prophet in Israel he spent much of his time roaming around the country, often visiting a place called Shunem. A rich local woman once invited him for supper with her husband. They must all have got on well, because after that they built a spare room on the roof for Elisha so that he'd always have somewhere to stay when he was passing that way. It was a pleasant little room, simply furnished with a bed, a table and chair, and a lamp. That was where Elisha always stayed, a quiet place where he could think and rest. It was exactly what he needed.

Elisha was most grateful to the woman who provided this safe place, and wanted to do something to help her. But no, she said. She had everything she wanted.

This wasn't strictly true. There was something she wanted very much. She hadn't said a word about it to Elisha, but his servant Gehazi knew.

"She and her husband can't have children," said Gehazi. "She wants a child so much, but it's not likely ever to happen."

Elisha called the woman to him. "At about this time next year," he said, "you will be cradling a son in your arms."

"Oh, sir, don't say that!" she cried. "Please, don't give me false hope!"

But it wasn't a false hope at all. A year later she gave birth to a beautiful son, and soon she and her husband couldn't imagine what life had been like without him. Like most small boys, he copied what his father did, so when his dad went out to the work in the fields, the little boy went with him. One morning when Elisha was away, the child was in the fields with his father and suddenly cried out, "My head! My head!"

The father caught the boy as he swayed and fell. The boy was carried indoors. The mother cradled her son on her lap, rocked him, and bathed his hot face and hands. Perhaps it was only too much sun, and he'd soon be better. He had to be. How could she live without him now?

The child nestled against her, not speaking nor moving. At noon, he died.

There was no time for crying. The mother knew at once what to do. She carried the child to Elisha's empty room, shut the door, and sent for a servant.

"I want to get to Elisha quickly, so I'll need a donkey," she said briskly. "He'll be at Mount Carmel, and I can be there and back in a day."

"Why do you need to see Elisha?" asked the servant. "It's not a religious festival today, is it?"

"All the same, I'm going," she said, and set a fast pace until they reached Mount Carmel. Gehazi came to meet them.

"Is anything the matter?" he asked.

"No, everything's all right at home," she said. "Just let me see Elisha, please."

When they reached Elisha she stopped pretending that everything was all right. In tears she threw herself at his feet and held on to him, though Gehazi tried to pull her away.

"Leave her alone!" ordered Elisha. "Can't you see she's very distressed? Let her tell me why."

"Sir, I didn't ask for a son!" she sobbed. "I begged you not to give me false hope! And now…"

She didn't have to say the rest. Elisha understood.

"Gehazi," he said, "take my staff and run all the way to the house. Don't stop for anything. When you get there, hold my staff over the boy."

"But I need you to come with me!" pleaded the woman, so she and Elisha followed Gehazi as he ran to the house. Gehazi got there first and held the staff across the child as Elisha had instructed, but nothing happened. The boy lay there, as still and cold as clay.

Elisha went in, shut the door, and prayed. He, too, tried to revive the boy. The child's body began to grow warm. Elisha kept praying and pacing the floor, then tried to revive him again.

Achoo! There was a violent sneeze from the little boy, then another, and another. After seven sneezes, he opened his eyes.

Elisha sent for the mother.

"Here he is!" he said, and for the second time that day she threw herself at his feet, but this time full of thanks. Then she took her little boy in her arms, alive and well.

Elisha continued Elijah's work, advising royalty and guiding the people of Israel through hard times of war and famine. He miraculously healed a Syrian general and saved a young family from being sold into slavery.

The Baby in the Temple

Here are some of the things most babies can and can't do at six weeks old.

They *can* —
> gurgle happily, and perhaps even smile;
> enjoy being cuddled and sung to;
> and recognize the faces and voices of the people they know.

They *can't* —
> sit up;
> talk;
> understand the words you say (but they can tell if your voice is kind);
> keep themselves warm or cool themselves down.

So when Jesus is taken to the Temple in Jerusalem at six weeks old he's wrapped snugly in a shawl, watching his mother Mary's face, which he thinks is the most beautiful thing in the world.

The Temple is vast, grand, and solemn. Mary and Joseph are taking him there because the laws of their religion require it, and they bring two white doves as an offering to God. The doves flutter and coo in their basket, and the baby turns his head to look.

Mary and Joseph must wait. They are not the only people at the Temple today. Others are there before them to say their prayers and make offerings, and these two poor people from the north must wait their turn. Mary hopes that it won't be too long, because in the next hour or two Jesus will need to be fed and changed. Where in this great and holy place could she clean up a baby?

An old man is approaching them, and in spite of his white hair and deeply wrinkled face he walks with a quick, sure step and his eyes twinkle with kindness. Mary is drawn to the warmth of his smile, and goes to meet him.

"Is this…" he begins, then looks down at Jesus. There is a pause, then he takes a deep breath.

"Yes," he says, and his voice cracks with joy and tears. "Yes, he is! This is the one! I can die a happy man now; I have seen my saviour – Israel's saviour – the bright light of all the world."

With a trembling finger he strokes Jesus' hair and looks into Mary's face.

"My dear, my name is Simeon, and I'm an old man," he says. "All my long life I have waited to see this child. He is the one."

Mary doesn't ask him how he knows. She has learned that God speaks to people in many ways.

"Would you like to hold him?" she asks, and places the child in Simeon's arms.

Jesus wriggles, stretches, and smiles at the kind face above him. He reaches up and curls his tiny fingers into the white beard.

"You, child, are the one who will bring God and his people together," says Simeon, rocking him. "You will draw the nations to God." He turns to Mary. "And for you, my dear, there will come a pain like a sword through your heart."

Mary doesn't want to think about that, not now. An old woman, stooping and slow on her feet, is coming to join them. She hesitates, and Joseph offers her his arm.

"Here's Anna!" says Simeon. "She's always in the Temple. Anna, come and see!"

Anna takes Jesus in her arms. A beautiful smile spreads across her face.

"It's you!" she says to the baby. "I'm eighty-four years old, and all my life I've waited for you!"

Other visitors to the Temple are squeezing past, and Anna shows all of them the baby. "Do you see this child?" she says. "The waiting is over, the messiah is here!"

A stirring of hunger makes Jesus uncomfortable and he cries, turning his head to Mary. Anna hands him back and he nestles against his mother, feeling safe in her warm, familiar arms.

All the way home Mary is quiet, and holds Jesus very close. She is turning over all the wonderful things that Simeon and Anna said, and the way they looked at Jesus.

And a sword will pierce your heart.

Whatever happens, I will protect him, she thinks. *God has trusted him to my care, and I will protect him. Or at least, every day of my life, I will try.*

There aren't many very old people in the Gospels. Here we have Simeon and Anna who had spent their long lives in worship and prayer. Simeon had been promised by God that he would live to see the messiah. Anna had been married and widowed young, and as she grew old she spent her whole life in the Temple. Perhaps they had learned to see people the way God sees them.

All her life, Mary did her best to protect Jesus. The time came when she couldn't, but she stood by him at the foot of the cross.

Blessing the Children

First there was just one woman, Becky and Josh's mother. She wanted Jesus to bless her children, so she took Becky and Josh and stood in the crowd around him. It was a sunny day so he was sitting outside to talk to everyone, and, same as always, there were hundreds of people around him. Some of them wanted to ask questions, some wanted healing or prayer, and some just wanted to hear the stories or find out what all the fuss was about. So Becky and Josh's mother had Becky by the hand and she had hoisted Josh up on to her shoulder so he could see.

My friend Lizzie and I could see the crowd around Jesus but we were busy playing weddings in the market square with all the other girls. (The boys didn't play weddings.) We were being the bridesmaids in the procession so we each took off one sandal and held it out like a bridesmaid's lamp, only it was really funny gazing at a scuffed old sandal as if it was shiny bright and weddingy, and besides it made us walk lopsided, so we had to be bridesmaids with limps. Lizzie got the giggles and it started us all off, so we didn't get very far with the wedding but it was fun. But then more of the women thought that Becky and Josh's mother had the right idea, so they were taking their children to see Jesus too, and our mothers came for us. Lizzie and I slipped our sandals back on quickly, thinking we'd be in trouble for getting our feet dirty. They weren't angry, they just said we were going to meet Jesus and we had to behave ourselves.

There was a queue, and I curled my toes with impatience as I waited. I'd never got near to Jesus of Nazareth before and it was a bit scary, because I didn't know what I'd say to him. Everyone said that he could heal ill people with a touch of his hand, but Lizzie and I weren't ill. We didn't need healing, but I was hoping for a story. Then two big men worked their way through the crowd, pushing us all back so firmly that Lizzie stepped on my foot.

"You're all crowding the master," they were saying. "Take the children away. No children. This isn't the place for them."

It was only then that I realized how much I wanted to see Jesus. Lizzie was saying "sorry, sorry!" and putting her arm around me – she thought I was crying because she'd trodden on my toes, but it wasn't that, I was crying because I was so disappointed. Then a voice rose, loud and strong, above everything else.

"Let the children through!" called Jesus. "Peter, John, what are you doing? Don't stop them!"

Everyone obeyed him. We were ushered through to the front, and suddenly we were all around Jesus with the little ones swarming onto his knee and into his arms. Lizzie and I sat near his feet. He was bearded and smiling, with kind eyes, and we couldn't be shy for long.

He didn't just talk, he listened, and we told him how we'd been playing weddings but the boys never joined in even if we played wedding music on little pipes, and he thought that was really funny. By the time he'd told us a story, said a prayer with us, and given us his blessing we felt as if he'd always been part of our lives.

The parents and grandparents were sitting around, too, and we all enjoyed his company.

When we had to leave, somebody – I think it was Becky and Josh's mother – told us to say thank you to Rabbi Jesus, so we did.

"Thank *you*," he said. And I could tell that he really meant it.

In Jesus' days, not everyone had a lot of time for children. But he did!

Beth, Daughter of Jairus

Sweat pours down Jairus's face. As he runs, his sandals slap on the hard road. The crowds block his way and he shoves and shoulders his way through. The people think, *This can't be Jairus! Has he gone mad? What's happened?*

Jairus is not the sort of man to run through the streets. He never pushes his way forward, he doesn't have to. He's one of the rulers of the synagogue, a man everyone respects, and today he wants to see Jesus of Nazareth. Everyone wants to see Jesus of Nazareth, but for Jairus it's urgent. The crowds have gathered around Jesus and those who can't see are stretching on tiptoe and looking for steps to climb up.

"I need your help! Please!" shouts Jairus. Finally, he stands before Jesus.

"Please, Rabbi Jesus, come with me," begs Jairus. "My daughter's very ill, my only daughter – she's dying, little Beth, she's dying. Please come, nobody else can help her!"

Jesus goes with him. As Jesus listens to what he has to say, Jairus has hope.

Beth has stopped twisting and rolling in her bed and lies still at last. Her mother fans a cool breeze across her face. It helps, but breathing is painful and difficult.

Now and again, she whimpers. The breeze is good, but it would be so much easier if she didn't have to breathe. She can hear voices, but can't see because her eyes are too heavy to open.

The crowds are still heaving around Jesus as he follows Jairus. Everybody wants his help, everyone tries to touch him.

"Let Rabbi Jesus through!" call the disciples, but they have to push to make a way for him. Suddenly he stops, and looks around.

"Who touched me?" he asks.

"In this crowd? Everyone's trying to touch you!" say the disciples.

"This way, sir," urges Jairus, but Jesus has turned from him. He is watching a thin, bright-eyed woman stepping nervously forward to kneel at his feet.

Beth sighs. She's done enough. Blackness washes gently over her but she isn't afraid of it, because it brushes the pain away. She lies feeling safe and peaceful as the sound of her mother's voice floats far beyond her. The pain has stopped. Everything has stopped. There is only peace and the feeling that she is waiting for something to happen.

Jairus stands still and feels the hope draining out of him. The woman is explaining to Jesus that for the last twelve years she has suffered from very bad bleeding, and none of the doctors she went to could help. Jesus' healing power has made her well. She reached out and touched him with faith, and that was enough.

Twelve years, thinks Jairus as his eyes fill with tears for his daughter. *Twelve years, all of Beth's lifetime. What a short time to live.* He is watching Jesus, desperate to catch his eye and remind him that Beth needs him, so he doesn't notice when one of his own servants arrives.

"Sir," says the servant quietly, and puts a gentle hand on his shoulder, "I'm so sorry. It's too late. Beth died just a few minutes ago. Come away, there's no point in staying here. It's all over, there's no need to bother Rabbi Jesus."

Jesus hears this and turns to them at once. "Lead the way, Jairus," he says. "Have faith."

They reach Jairus's house to find the family and friends in tears. Mourners are outside, lamenting loudly and playing their mournful music.

"There's no need for that," says Jesus firmly. "She isn't dead, she's just asleep."

At first they laugh at him, but when he tells them to go away they do as he says without arguing. Peter, James and John, and Jairus go with him into the room where she lies.

Beth's mother is still at her bedside. She no longer fans Beth's face. Again and again she has felt for a pulse, and found nothing. Now she holds her daughter in her arms, meaning to hold her until the last warmth leaves her child's body.

"May I?" asks Jesus, and takes Beth's hand. It looks frail and lifeless in his weathered brown fingers.

"Up you get now, child," he says kindly.

At first nothing seems to happen, then a bright wave of joy and health surges

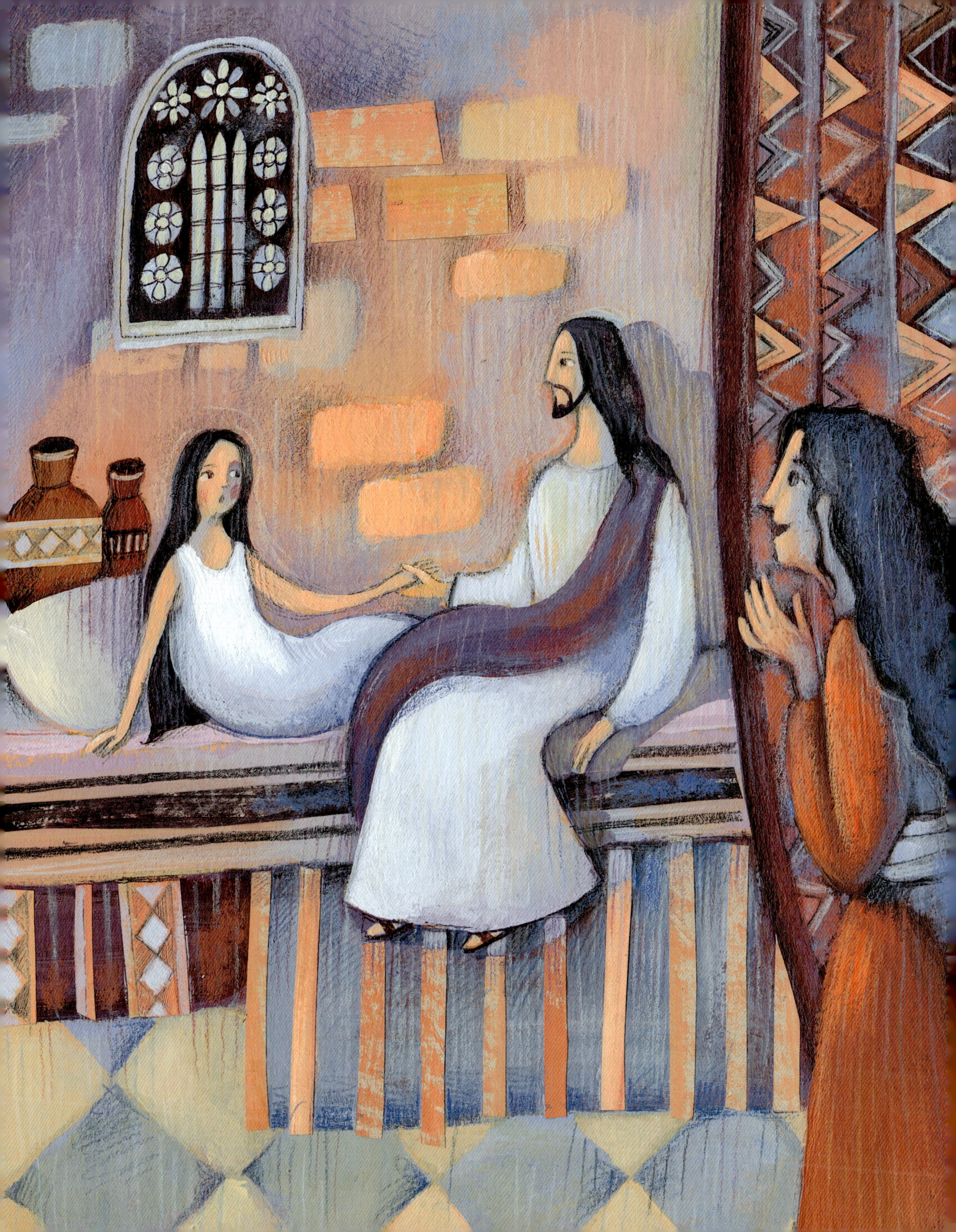

through Beth, so she opens her eyes and sits up. A man is smiling down at her and she feels she's seen him somewhere before, quite recently. She feels well, happy, hungry, and ready to get out of bed.

"Give her something to eat," says Jesus, so gratefully her mother goes to sort out some bread and soup. As he leaves, Jesus tells them, "Don't tell anyone about this."

It's a bit late for that, thinks Jairus. He's just seen Beth running to the window to wave to her friends in the street.

This story says a lot about Jesus. He gave one-to-one attention to the woman and to Beth, in spite of all the crowds thronging about him. "Give her something to eat" sounds like very sensible advice, too.

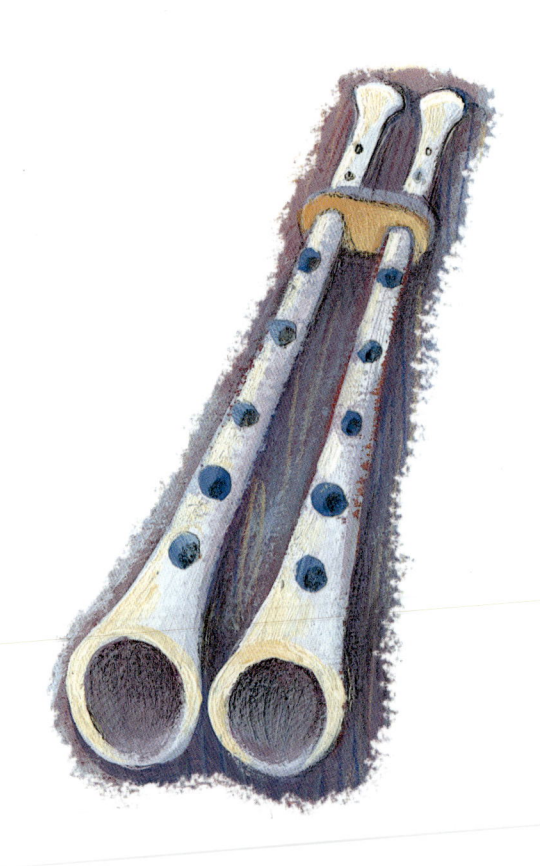

Bread and Fishes

MARK'S MOTHER LOVED to cook, and did it, as Mark's dad used to say, "with a generous hand". She always made a bit extra because she said that children needed feeding up, and she made a bit more after that in case anybody arrived unexpectedly. It was cheap, simple food, but it was always very good and everyone enjoyed it. Sometimes, if the weather had been bad and the harvests poor, even Mark's mother couldn't feed the family as well as she'd like. The soup might be thin and the bread might have bits of barley husk in it to make it go further. Fortunately they lived near the lake and they all liked fish.

At a time when the weather, the fish, and the bread were all pretty good, a rabbi was going around the towns and villages with his twelve assistants, or "disciples" as they were called. Mark's dad said that if they turned up in their village Mama would round them up, sit them at the table, and not let them preach until they'd worked their way through soup, bread, three kinds of fish, wheat salad, and honeyed figs for afters.

Rabbi Jesus and his disciples did come by, but not to their village. The word spread that they were on their way up a hill near the lake, so if you wanted to hear him you had to make an effort. For Mark, it was worth that effort. He'd heard about Jesus of Nazareth. Everyone had heard of Jesus of Nazareth, who worked miracles, told good stories, and talked about God in a way nobody else did.

"I'd like to go up and hear him myself," said Mark's mother as she packed some lunch into a basket. "Tell me all about it when you get back."

"Mama!" said Mark, watching her pack another loaf. "I can't eat all that!"

"You don't know how long you're going to be out," she replied. "Fresh mountain air gives you an appetite, and if any of your friends are there…" she pushed another roll in, "you'll need something to share."

By the time Mark left the house he was carrying five loaves and two fishes. He was young and good at scrambling up hills, so he was one of the first to sit down on a rock, ready to listen to Jesus. He considered eating one of the rolls to be going on with — but when Jesus started talking Mark forgot about food, and everything else. Nobody had ever talked about God like this! As Mark listened, he felt that God was really here with them and enjoying their company. All the time the crowd grew as more and more people — men, women, and children — came to join them.

Jesus was such a good teacher, and such a brilliant storyteller, that time passed quickly. Mark only knew he'd been there a long time when his stomach growled and he had to press his hand against it to stop it from doing it again. A squint up at the sky told him that it must be long after midday. Presently, Jesus paused in his teaching and stopped to have a quiet word with his disciples, who kept turning around to gaze anxiously at the crowd.

Mark looked over his shoulder and gasped in surprise. There must have been thousands of people there, and that was only the adults!

Hungry, he unwrapped his packed lunch — then he stopped. This was awkward. Other people might not have brought food, and it would be bad manners to eat in front of them. Sharing was all very well, but there were too

34

many people on either side and behind him, and it wouldn't go around them all.

Jesus would know what to do, thought Mark. He'd like to ask him. And then it dawned upon him, very simply and clearly, that he could. He could ask him anything! There was nothing to stop him talking to Jesus – except that Jesus was still talking with his disciples and Mark didn't like to interrupt. All the same, he got up and made his way to the little cluster of men. He caught the odd word and understood that the disciples were worried about food, too, surveying the crowd and scrabbling about for the few pennies they had between them. (Mark could have told them that money wouldn't help. The nearest baker was two miles away and he'd have sold out and closed by now.)

Oh, well... Mark had always been taught to share. He knew now what he wanted to do. He couldn't help all these people, but he could share with Rabbi Jesus, who looked thin around the face as if he could do with a good meal. In need of feeding up, Mama would have said. And that was when one of Jesus' friends – it turned out to be Andrew the fisherman – noticed him. Mark felt suddenly shy, but he managed to say, "I want to share this with Jesus – um – please, sir."

Andrew smiled down at him and steered him through the close little group of worried disciples.

"There's a lad here with five loaves and two fishes, Lord," he said. "He wants to share them with you."

Mark, knowing that the disciples were all looking at him, felt his face redden. He hoped they weren't expecting to share his meal too – there'd only be enough for a mouthful each, and it was his lunch, after all. He pushed the basket toward Jesus, who smiled broadly as he took it.

"That," said Jesus, "is exactly what we need! Andrew, Philip, get everyone to sit down in groups, so you can get around them. What's your name?"

"Mark," he said.

"Mark, let's give thanks to God," said Jesus.

Jesus closed his eyes, became very still, then said a prayer of thanksgiving. When he took a roll in both hands and broke it, the smell of fresh bread made Mark's stomach yawn with hunger.

"Here you are, Mark," said Jesus, putting half a loaf and a bit of fish into his hands. "Philip, John, see if anyone has any baskets we can use."

Mark was enjoying the bread and picking crumbs off his tunic, so he didn't quite see how it happened, but when he looked up Jesus was still breaking bread and handing it out. Fish, too. He turned to see where the disciples were and saw that they were moving through the crowd and giving out bread and fish. How could…?

"There won't be any left for you, sir," said Mark and offered half of his fish to Jesus who thanked him, ate it, and went on sharing out food. There was even more of it now! The disciples were breaking bread and passing it around. Adults were sharing bread with their children; children were licking bits of fish from their fingers. Andrew had worked his way to the back of the crowd and the food still hadn't run out. Everyone ate. Everything was shared. Mark would have liked to ask Jesus how he did it but his mouth was always full. And just as he felt comfortably and pleasantly that he'd had enough, Peter gave him an empty basket and said, "Help us to clear up the crumbs, will you, son?"

By the time they had cleared up there were twelve baskets of crumbs and broken rolls. Mark began the long walk home, munching a bit of leftover bread as he went. At home, his mother put a bowl of soup in front of him.

"Tell me all about it, then," she said.

"Something amazing happened," replied Mark. Between mouthfuls of soup he told her about the teaching and stories, and then said, "I took my lunch to share with Jesus, and that was when the something amazing started. You know how you always make a little bit of food go a long way…?"

There are different versions of this story in the Bible. You might like to look it up in chapter six of John's Gospel. It's one of those stories that shows how Jesus cares about our ordinary needs.

The loaves in this story weren't as big as the ones we usually buy today, nor the same shape. They might have been like small baguettes, or round and flat.

The Child in the Middle

I'M HANNAH, I live in Capernaum, and I want to tell you about something that happened when Jesus came to stay. The day was like a great big party. Long before anyone arrived I was running around getting under everyone's feet, showing off how good I was at organising things – "I'll get bowls of water for foot washing, I'll fold some towels," and all that. I was eleven and doing my helpful "eldest daughter" bit. Our little Zack was under everyone's feet too, but Zackie was two years old, big-eyed, curly-haired, and as adorable as a puppy.

Jesus and his friends were coming to Capernaum, and he'd sent his disciples James and John ahead to ask if they could stay with us. Capernaum was the place he always came back to and we had lots of room in our house, so of course Ma said it would be fine (with me whispering, "Say yes! Say yes!" in her ear). Even though we were used to him in our town, we never took him for granted. As soon as he showed his face, he was mobbed. Even the people who didn't like him came to see him, just so they could ask him trick questions and try to catch him out, or because they were having arguments with their families and wanted him to sort it out for them, but he wouldn't. He always got them to do it for themselves.

Mostly, people went to him for one of two things – healing or teaching, and the teaching was mostly in stories. Usually I'd be hanging around for the stories, but this time I was helping to get everything ready at home. I put bread and figs on the table.

"I do," said Zackie, toddling around after me. "I do dat, Hanni."

"You do it, then," I said. He was such a poppet! "I do dat," meant "I'll do that," which was Zack's way of saying that he wanted to help. He wanted to do whatever he saw me doing – setting or clearing tables, hanging out washing, even brushing my hair. "I do, I do, Hanni." He'd trot about fetching and carrying, and he was so funny. Sometimes I'd tease him, but just gently. He saw me filling a jug of wine to put on the table.

"I do dat!" he said. "I do."

"Go on, then," I said, and watched him try to pick it up with his two chubby little hands. It didn't move. He tried again, and gave up.

"Hanni do it," he said, and that was the pattern for the rest of the day. Anything too heavy to lift or a heap of towels he couldn't see over, it was "Hanni do". So I did. He thought that plumping up the big cushions was the greatest fun ever, so I left him to it while I set tables, then I turned around and he'd disappeared.

"Oof!" said a voice from somewhere under a cushion. We all fell about laughing and Zack didn't understand why but he knew he must have done something funny, so he giggled, crawled out, and fell down on a cushion on purpose. Eventually he grew tired and a bit grumpy and put his arms up to be carried, so I put him on my hip and as soon as he was being held he rubbed his eyes and became droopy, so I sat and cuddled him until he fell asleep in my lap. I loved it when he did that. He was so warm and trusting in his sleep. I had two other brothers who thought they were God's gift to the people of Israel, but I loved my baby brother, Zack, best.

Zack was still pink, rosy, and asleep when Jesus and his disciples arrived in the marketplace. I knew Jesus was there; I could hear all the commotion outside as people ran, or limped, or were carried to meet him. I would have gone out, too, but I didn't want to disturb Zack. There'd be time enough to listen to Jesus when he came to our house.

By the time they all came in – Jesus and his friends – Zack was awake again and his usual happy self, staring with wide eyes at all the visitors. Jesus asked for God's blessing on our house and we all took bowls of water and towels for the foot washing. I moved pretty quickly because I wanted to be the one who did Jesus' feet, so Zack toddled after me singing out "I do! I do, Hanni!", and dabbed at Jesus' toes with a bit of towel. Then Zack tried to lift up the bowl of water, changed his mind, and said, "Hanni do," but it was Jesus who picked it up for me and handed it to one of the servants. (He used to say that we should all serve each other.) Then he turned to his friends, who were all chatting away, and said quite casually,

"What were you all talking about on the way here?"

They were suddenly quiet. They all looked down at their sandals, looked at each other, looked as if they'd rather be somewhere else, then muttered things like "nothing much", and "er…". Jesus helped them out.

"You were talking about which of you is the most important," he said. "Isn't that right?"

"Yes, Rabbi," they said sheepishly, and looked down again at their (very clean) feet.

"And what did you decide?" he asked. "Who do you think is the most important? Peter? James, John? Judas? Is it you?"

Nobody wanted to answer, and he didn't push them. Instead he clapped his hands and held out his arms to Zack, who ran straight to him like a bird to a nest. Jesus swung him on to his knee, and Zack sat there quite happily with one little soft hand on Jesus' arm.

"Do you see this child?" said Jesus. "He's the most important in the kingdom of heaven. Unless you come to me as simply and trustingly as this little boy you'll never understand what I'm doing. Zack here is the greatest in the kingdom of heaven. Peter, James, John, Judas, all of you, try to understand that!"

And all the time Zack just sat there, in the middle of them all, looking up at Jesus and stroking his beard to see what it felt like.

Little children, even cute ones like Zack, can be annoying sometimes, but at heart they just want to love and be loved. I often think about that day, and Zack, and think again about what it was about him that made Jesus say those words, *"the greatest in the kingdom of heaven"*.

Helen, the Jailer's Daughter

When you tell your friends that you live at the prison, they don't want to come to your house. My friends never came to call; perhaps their parents wouldn't let them.

We don't actually live in the prison, we have the house beside it because my dad is the head jailer. What's the matter with that? Somebody has to make sure that violent criminals are locked up. The only thing is that the Romans are in charge and they're not that fussy about who they lock up. That's not the worst of it. If a prisoner escapes, the jailer is put to death. Can you imagine that, knowing that a mistake at work could kill you? No wonder Dad looked so grim all the time. He kept all his prisoners chained up, just in case. But that particular night – the night when everything changed – the prisoners weren't trying to escape at all. They were singing all night, and saying prayers!

The prisoners were called Paul and Silas and they had come from Jerusalem. They hadn't even done anything bad. They came to town to tell people about God, and while they were there they set free a poor confused girl who was forced to work as a fortune teller. She didn't get to keep the money she earned. The men who controlled her took all of her earnings, so when Paul and Silas set her free the men were livid. They started a riot, blamed Paul and Silas for it, and got them arrested.

The soldiers gave Paul and Silas a beating that left them bleeding and covered in bruises, and from my window I saw them being dragged off to prison — and yes, I do mean dragged, they could barely walk. I wished I hadn't seen that, because I couldn't un-see it. That picture of them stayed in my head.

It was still there when I went to bed, and I couldn't sleep. I lay awake unhappily, waiting for sleep or for morning, until at last I began to drift off. Then my bed rocked.

I sat up straight, holding on to the sides of my bed in terror as everything shook. The movement, rumbles, and crashes sent me staggering to my mother's room, but she was coming to find me and I fell into her arms.

"Are the gods angry?" I gasped.

"It's an earthquake," she said, grabbing my hand as she ran from the house. "Only a small one, if the gods are merciful."

My brothers ran out too and we waited outside, standing well back from the house. When it had been quiet for a while, Ma said it should be safe to go back inside, then — and I still feel that surge of excitement when I think about it — then we heard Dad laughing! He was on his way from the prison with those two men, Paul and Silas, no chains or anything, and the three of them smiling all over their faces!

That was the moment when I *knew* I must be dreaming, because things like that only happen in dreams. The earth shakes. Dad comes home in the middle of the night with two injured, bruised, and very happy prisoners, except they're not in prison! This could not be real. If I'd turned into a tree I wouldn't have been at all surprised.

But it was all really happening! Dad called for food, drink, hot water, and towels, and we all ran around lighting lamps and tripping over each other to get food and things together. It was the most exciting thing that had happened in our house in years. Dad washed Paul and Silas's wounds, and they all told us what had happened.

Paul and Silas, instead of moaning about how unfair everything was, had been praying and singing to their God when the earthquake shook the cell. Their chains had just dropped away from them! Dad had gone rushing in, terrified that they'd escape, because you know what that would mean, but Paul and Silas weren't going anywhere. They made no attempt at all to escape, just stood there reassuring Dad that they wouldn't run away. He was so impressed that he brought them home as welcomed guests.

Paul and Silas talked freely and easily, and I loved them for making Dad happier than I'd seen him in years. I kept quiet because if Ma and Dad forgot that I was there they wouldn't send me back to bed, and I wanted to stay up. Those men so clearly loved their Christ, and wanted everyone to know him. I didn't understand half of what they said, but I wanted to be like them with their joy and faith. I realized how much the closed, fearful atmosphere of prison had got into me, and I wanted to be free from it. When they started talking about baptism I realized it was what I wanted – I couldn't wait to plunge down into the water and come up feeling fresh and clean. "Helen, I baptize you…" said Silas, and my own name sounded like a breath of spring.

And what happened next?

In the morning
Paul and Silas were given an official
pardon because they were Roman citizens and
shouldn't have been arrested in the first place. They went away after
that, but they'd already established a group of believers around here, and some
of them had families. Suddenly I had more friends than ever before, real friends
who didn't mind coming to the jailer's house and weren't afraid. We all knew
the difference between prison and freedom.

The Bible doesn't say anything else about the jailer's family, but we know that Paul and Silas started a Christian community in Philippi, where they lived. This means they would have friends who shared their beliefs.

Paul and Silas journeyed from one town to another — Ephesus, Philippi, Galatia, Corinth — preaching and healing. They would set up Christian communities, and Paul would revisit them when he could. In the meantime, he wrote to them. Most of what we know about Paul's thinking and teaching is in these letters, or "epistles".